About the Learn Any Foreign Language Handbook

This handbook is designed for students who want to begin studying a foreign language. This is a unique and creative approach which can be used alone or alongside other language curricula such as Rosetta Stone, Pimsleur, or other online programs.

Students will research new words and phrases, then memorize and practice them in in a fun way.

Activities include:

- Movie Time: Watching films and documentaries and videos in a foreign language
- Research words and phrases used in different types of conversation and situations
- Make your own comics in the foreign language
- Get creative with text message conversations
- And More!

Supplies Needed:

To complete this guided learning handbook, students will need books, notebooks and pencils, a foreign language/English dictionary or Google Translate, and access to the Internet for films/documentaries. This journal can be used daily for an intensive language learning unit lasting about a month or once a week to last all school year.

The Thinking Tree

Learn Any FOREIGN Language

Handbook for Students

Anna Miriam Brown

Sarah Janisse Brown

Copyright 2019

The Thinking Tree, LLC

FunSchooling.com

Topics covered in this book:

- Food
- Transportation
- Compliments
- Animals
- Cooking
- Human Anatomy
- Sports
- Happiness
- World Travel
- Money and Finance
- Common Courtesy
- Greetings
- Space
- Colors
- Human Body
- Illness
- The Holidays
- Music
- Directions
- Insults
- Family
- Clothing
- Entertainment
- Saying Sorry
- Emotions
- Sadness
- Shame
- Anger
- Worry
- Excitement
- Nervousness
- Politics
- Society
- Jokes
- Religion
- Art
- Bills and Coins
- Coffee & Tea
- Compliments
- Home
- Electronics
- Weather
- Dancing
- Nature
- Math/Measurements
- Seasons
- Numbers
- Shopping
- Sayings/Quotes
- Date & Time
- Emergencies

My New Language:

_____

Country of Origin:

_____

MOVIE TIME!

Watch a film, documentary, or YouTube video in your new language

Title: ....
....
Producer: ....
....
Actors: ....
....
....

10 WORDS

Write down 10 words you hear while watching the film.

Foreign Language	English
1._____	1._____
2._____	2._____
3._____	3._____
4._____	4._____
5._____	5._____
6._____	6._____
7._____	7._____
8._____	8._____
9._____	9._____
10._____	10._____

RATING:

The Best

Amazing

Good

Nice

Ok

Bad

Horrible

The Worst

FOOD
10 NEW WORDS!

> Use a book, video, or Google Translate to find your ten words.

Foreign Language	English
_____	_____
_____	_____
_____	_____
_____	_____
_____	_____
_____	_____
_____	_____
_____	_____
_____	_____
_____	_____

Research ten words you might use in a conversation about food.

> After you've written your words, say them each seven times out loud, picturing them in your mind.

Research Time!

FIVE NEW PHRASES!

Research five phrases you might use in a conversation about food.

1. ___Foreign Language_____

___English_____

_____

2. _____

_____

_____

3. _____

_____

_____

4. _____

_____

_____

5. _____

_____

After you've written your phrases, say them each seven times out loud, picturing them in your mind.

The Fun Page

Fruits and Veggies

It's research time! Find and translate your 10 favorite fruits and vegetables.

After you've written your words, say them each seven times out loud, picturing them in your mind.

Foreign Language	English
1._____	1._____
2._____	2._____
3._____	3._____
4._____	4._____
5._____	5._____
6._____	6._____
7._____	7._____
8._____	8._____
9._____	9._____
10._____	10._____

Illustrate what you've learned.

Add Words to the Doodle

**Find words to describe this picture.
Add your words to this page in a creative way.**

Make Your Own Texts

Using inspiration from the previous pages,
make your own text conversation in _____.

After you've finished, read your conversation aloud seven times.

MOVIE TIME!

Watch a film, documentary, or YouTube video in your new language

Title: ....
....
Producer: ....
....
Actors: ....
....
....

10 WORDS

Write down 10 words you hear while watching the film.

Foreign Language	English
1._____	1._____
2._____	2._____
3._____	3._____
4._____	4._____
5._____	5._____
6._____	6._____
7._____	7._____
8._____	8._____
9._____	9._____
10._____	10._____

RATING:

The Best

Amazing

Great

Good

Nice

Ok

Bad

Horrible

The Worst

TRANSPORTATION
10 NEW WORDS!

Use a book, video, or Google Translate to find your ten words.

Foreign Language　　　　　**English**

_____　　_____

_____　　_____

_____　　_____

_____　　_____

_____　　_____

_____　　_____

_____　　_____

_____　　_____

_____　　_____

_____　　_____

Research ten words you might use in a conversation about transportation.

After you've written your words, say them each seven times out loud, picturing them in your mind.

Research Time!

FIVE NEW PHRASES!

Research five phrases you might use in a conversation about transportation.

1. Foreign Language _____

English _____

_____

2. _____

_____

3. _____

_____

4. _____

_____

5. _____

_____

After you've written your phrases, say them each seven times out loud, picturing them in your mind.

The Fun Page

Translate five compliments and practice them!

1. Foreign Language _____
   English _____

2. _____
   _____

3. _____
   _____

4. _____
   _____

5. _____
   _____

After you've written these sentences, say them each seven times out loud, picturing them in your mind.

Illustrate what you've learned.

Make Your Own Comic

Using inspiration from the previous pages, make your own comic in your new language.

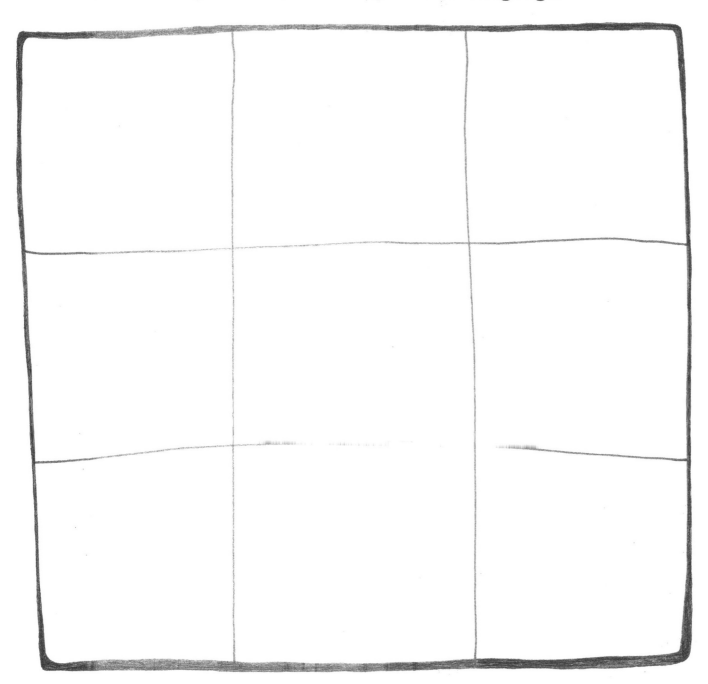

After you've finished, read your comic aloud seven times.

Make Your Own Texts

Using inspiration from the previous pages, make your own text conversation in your new language.

After you've finished, read your conversation aloud seven times.

MOVIE TIME!

Watch a film, documentary, or YouTube video in your new language

Title: ....
....
Producer: ....
....
Actors: ....
....
....

10 WORDS

Write down 10 words you hear while watching the film.

Foreign Language

1. _____
2. _____
3. _____
4. _____
5. _____
6. _____
7. _____
8. _____
9. _____
10. _____

English

1. _____
2. _____
3. _____
4. _____
5. _____
6. _____
7. _____
8. _____
9. _____
10. _____

RATING:

The Best

Amazing

Great

Good

Nice

Ok

Bad

Horrible

The Worst

ANIMALS
10 NEW WORDS!

Use a book, video, or Google Translate to find your ten words.

Foreign Language	English
_____	_____
_____	_____
_____	_____
_____	_____
_____	_____
_____	_____
_____	_____
_____	_____
_____	_____
_____	_____

Research ten words you might use in a conversation about animals.

After you've written your words, say them each seven times out loud, picturing them in your mind.

Research Time!

FIVE NEW PHRASES!

Research five phrases you might use in a conversation about animals.

1. Foreign Language _____
   English _____

2. _____

3. _____

4. _____

5. _____

After you've written your phrases, say them each seven times out loud, picturing them in your mind.

The Fun Page

Find a recipe originating from a place where the language you're studying is spoken. Translate the recipe and copy it down here.

What's cooking? _____

Instructions Below:

After you've written the recipe, read it aloud seven times, picturing them in your mind.

Now, get cooking!

Illustrate what you've learned.

Add Words to the Doodle

**Find words to describe this picture.
Add your words to this page in a creative way.**

Make Your Own Texts

Using inspiration from the previous pages,
make your own text conversation in _____ .

After you've finished, read your conversation aloud seven times.

MOVIE TIME!

Watch a film, documentary, or YouTube video in your new language

Title: ....
....
Producer: ....
....
Actors: ....
....
....

10 WORDS

Write down 10 words you hear while watching the film.

Foreign Language

1. _____
2. _____
3. _____
4. _____
5. _____
6. _____
7. _____
8. _____
9. _____
10. _____

English

1. _____
2. _____
3. _____
4. _____
5. _____
6. _____
7. _____
8. _____
9. _____
10. _____

RATING:

The Best

Amazing

Great

Good

Nice

Ok

Bad

Horrible

The Worst

HUMAN ANATOMY
10 NEW WORDS!

Use a book, video, or Google Translate to find your ten words.

Foreign Language   **English**

_____   _____

_____   _____

_____   _____

_____   _____

_____   _____

_____   _____

_____   _____

_____   _____

_____   _____

_____   _____

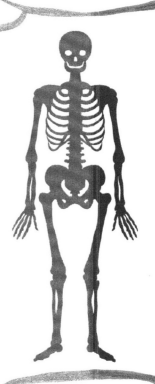

Research ten words you might use in a conversation about human anatomy.

After you've written your words, say them each seven times out loud, picturing them in your mind.

Research Time!

FIVE NEW PHRASES!

Research five phrases you might use in a conversation about human anatomy.

1. _Foreign Language_ _____

   English _____

2. _____

3. _____

4. _____

5. _____

After you've written your phrases, say them each seven times out loud, picturing them in your mind.

The Fun Page

Do a search on this language's most used words, or guess!

After you've written your words, say them each seven times out loud, picturing them in your mind.

Foreign Language | English
1._____ 1._____
2._____ 2._____
3._____ 3._____
4._____ 4._____
5._____ 5._____
6._____ 6._____
7._____ 7._____
8._____ 8._____
9._____ 9._____
10._____ 10._____

Illustrate what you've learned.

Make Your Own Comic

Using inspiration from the previous pages, make your own comic in your new language.

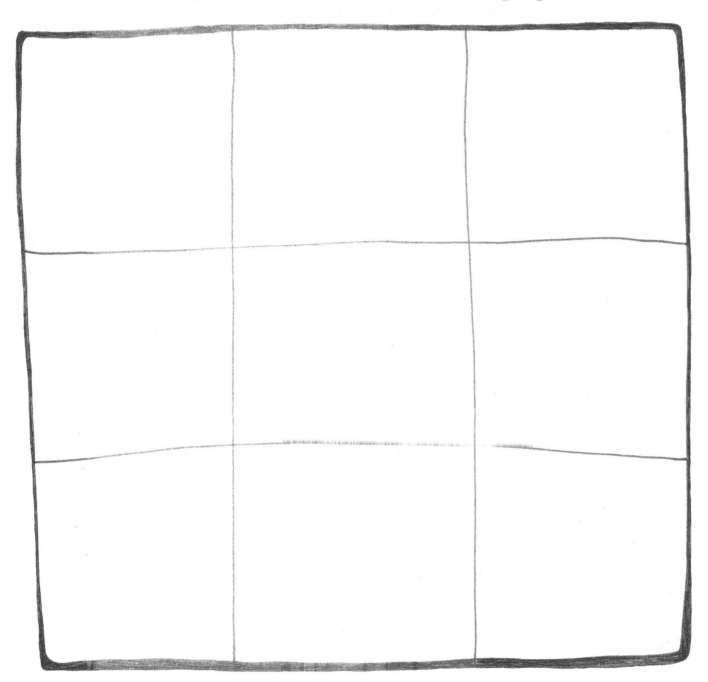

After you've finished, read your comic aloud seven times.

Make Your Own Texts

Using inspiration from the previous pages, make your own text conversation in your new language.

After you've finished, read your conversation aloud seven times.

MOVIE TIME!

Watch a film, documentary, or YouTube video in your new language

Title: ....
....
Producer: ....
....
Actors: ....
....
....

10 WORDS

Write down 10 words you hear while watching the film.

Foreign Language

1. _____
2. _____
3. _____
4. _____
5. _____
6. _____
7. _____
8. _____
9. _____
10. _____

English

1. _____
2. _____
3. _____
4. _____
5. _____
6. _____
7. _____
8. _____
9. _____
10. _____

RATING:

The Best

Amazing

Great

Good

Nice

Ok

Bad

Horrible

The Worst

SPORTS
10 NEW WORDS!

Use a book, video, or Google Translate to find your ten words.

Foreign Language	English
_____	_____
_____	_____
_____	_____
_____	_____
_____	_____
_____	_____
_____	_____
_____	_____
_____	_____
_____	_____

Research ten words you might use in a conversation about sports.

After you've written your words, say them each seven times out loud, picturing them in your mind.

Research Time!

FIVE NEW PHRASES!

Research five phrases you might use in a conversation about sports.

1. __Foreign Language_____
   __English_____
   _____

2. _____
   _____
   _____

3. _____
   _____
   _____

4. _____

5. _____
   _____

After you've written your phrases, say them each seven times out loud, picturing them in your mind.

The Fun Page

EMOTIONAL TALK: Happiness

Write five phrases you might say when you're happy.

1. __Foreign Language_____
   __English_____

2. _____
   _____

3. _____
   _____

4. _____
   _____

5. _____
   _____

After you've written these sentences, say them each seven times out loud, picturing them in your mind.

Illustrate what you've learned.

Make Your Own Comic

Using inspiration from the previous pages, make your own comic in _____.

After you've finished, read your comic aloud seven times.

Add Words to the Doodle

**Find words to describe this picture.
Add your words to this page in a creative way.**

MOVIE TIME!

Watch a film, documentary, or YouTube video in your new language

Title: ....
....
Producer: ....
....
Actors: ....
....
....

10 WORDS

Write down 10 words you hear while watching the film.

Foreign Language

1. _____
2. _____
3. _____
4. _____
5. _____
6. _____
7. _____
8. _____
9. _____
10. _____

English

1. _____
2. _____
3. _____
4. _____
5. _____
6. _____
7. _____
8. _____
9. _____
10. _____

RATING:

The Best

Amazing

Great

Nice

Ok

Bad

Horrible

The Worst

WORLD TRAVEL
10 NEW WORDS!

Use a book, video, or Google Translate to find your ten words.

Foreign Language **English**

_____ _____

_____ _____

_____ _____

_____ _____

_____ _____

_____ _____

_____ _____

_____ _____

_____ _____

_____ _____

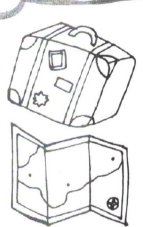

Research ten words you might use in a conversation about world travel.

After you've written your words, say them each seven times out loud, picturing them in your mind.

Research Time!

FIVE NEW PHRASES!

Research five phrases you might use in a conversation about world travel.

1. _Foreign Language_ _____
   English _____

2. _____
   _____

3. _____
   _____

4. _____
   _____

5. _____
   _____

After you've written your phrases, say them each seven times out loud, picturing them in your mind.

The Fun Page

Challenge yourself to only talk in _____ for the next hour. Write down five sentences you plan to use.

1. ___Foreign Language_____
   ___English_____

2. _____
   _____

3. _____
   _____

4. _____
   _____

5. _____
   _____

After you've written these sentences, say them each seven times out loud, picturing them in your mind.

Illustrate what you've learned.

Add Words to the Doodle

Find words to describe this picture.
Add your words to this page in a creative way.

Make Your Own Texts

Using inspiration from the previous pages, make your own text conversation in your new language.

After you've finished, read your conversation aloud seven times.

MOVIE TIME!

Watch a film, documentary, or YouTube video in your new language

Title: ....
....
Producer: ....
....
Actors: ....
....
....

10 WORDS

Write down 10 words you hear while watching the film.

Foreign Language　　　　　　　**English**

1. _____　　1. _____
2. _____　　2. _____
3. _____　　3. _____
4. _____　　4. _____
5. _____　　5. _____
6. _____　　6. _____
7. _____　　7. _____
8. _____　　8. _____
9. _____　　9. _____
10. _____　　10. _____

RATING:

The Best

Amazing

Great

Good

Nice

Ok

Bad

Horrible

The Worst

MONEY AND FINANCE
10 NEW WORDS!

Use a book, video, or Google Translate to find your ten words.

Foreign Language	English
_____	_____
_____	_____
_____	_____
_____	_____
_____	_____
_____	_____
_____	_____
_____	_____
_____	_____
_____	_____

Research ten words you might use in a conversation about money and finance.

After you've written your words, say them each seven times out loud, picturing them in your mind.

Research Time!

FIVE NEW PHRASES!

Research five phrases you might use in a conversation about money and finance.

1. Foreign Language _____
   English _____

2. _____

3. _____

4. _____

5. _____

After you've written your phrases, say them each seven times out loud, picturing them in your mind.

The Fun Page

Study the Money

Draw a few bills and coins from a place where this language is spoken.

Who is on the money? One interesting fact to research is who are the people that country puts on their bills.

Make Your Own Comic

Using inspiration from the previous pages, make your own comic in your new language.

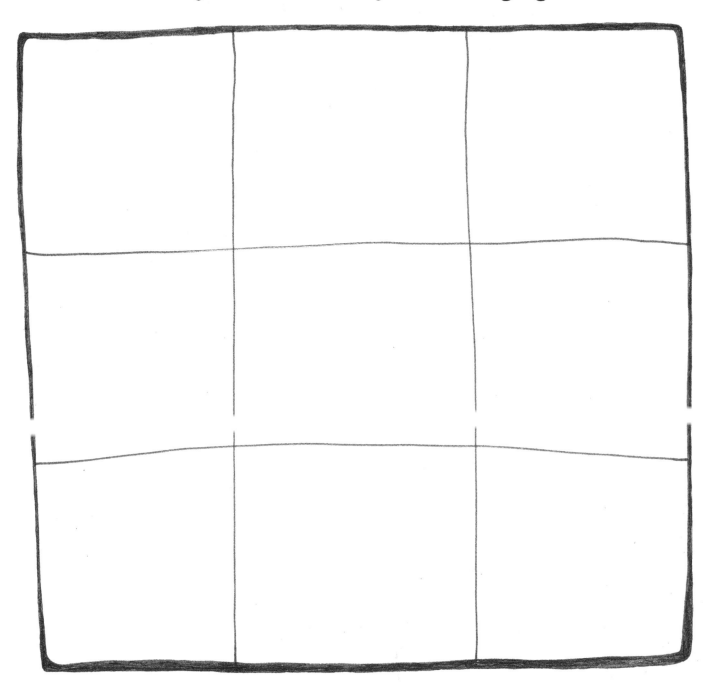

After you've finished, read your comic aloud seven times.

Make Your Own Texts

Using inspiration from the previous pages, make your own text conversation in _____ .

After you've finished, read your conversation aloud seven times.

MOVIE TIME!

Watch a film, documentary, or YouTube video in your new language

Title: ....
....
Producer: ....
....
Actors: ....
....
....

10 WORDS

Write down 10 words you hear while watching the film.

Foreign Language	English
1._____	1._____
2._____	2._____
3._____	3._____
4._____	4._____
5._____	5._____
6._____	6._____
7._____	7._____
8._____	8._____
9._____	9._____
10._____	10._____

RATING:

The Best

Amazing

Great

Nice

Ok

Bad

Horrible

The Worst

COMMON COURTESY
10 NEW WORDS!

Use a book, video, or Google Translate to find your ten words.

Foreign Language   **English**

_____   _____

_____   _____

_____   _____

_____   _____

_____   _____

_____   _____

_____   _____

_____   _____

_____   _____

_____   _____

Research ten words you might use in a conversation about common courtesy.

After you've written your words, say them each seven times out loud, picturing them in your mind.

Research Time!

FIVE NEW PHRASES!

Research five phrases you might use in a conversation about common courtesy.

1. Foreign Language _____

   English _____

2. _____

   _____

3. _____

   _____

4. _____

   _____

5. _____

   _____

After you've written your phrases, say them each seven times out loud, picturing them in your mind.

The Fun Page

Greetings! Do research and write down five common greetings.

1. _Foreign Language_ _____
   English _____

2. _____
   _____

3. _____
   _____

4. _____
   _____

5. _____
   _____

After you've written these sentences, say them each seven times out loud, picturing them in your mind.

Illustrate what you've learned.

Make Your Own Comic

Using inspiration from the previous pages, make your own comic in _____ .

After you've finished, read your comic aloud seven times.

Add Words to the Doodle

**Find words to describe this picture.
Add your words to this page in a creative way.**

MOVIE TIME!

Watch a film, documentary, or YouTube video in your new language

Title: ....
....
Producer: ....
....
Actors: ....
....
....

10 WORDS

Write down 10 words you hear while watching the film.

Foreign Language

1. _____
2. _____
3. _____
4. _____
5. _____
6. _____
7. _____
8. _____
9. _____
10. _____

English

1. _____
2. _____
3. _____
4. _____
5. _____
6. _____
7. _____
8. _____
9. _____
10. _____

RATING:

The Best

Amazing

Great

Good

Nice

Ok

Bad

Horrible

The Worst

SPACE
10 NEW WORDS!

Use a book, video, or Google Translate to find your ten words.

Foreign Language   **English**

_____ _____
_____ _____
_____ _____
_____ _____
_____ _____
_____ _____
_____ _____
_____ _____
_____ _____
_____ _____

Research ten words you might use in a conversation about space.

After you've written your words, say them each seven times out loud, picturing them in your mind.

Research Time!

FIVE NEW PHRASES!

Research five phrases you might use in a conversation about space.

1. ___Foreign Language_____
   ___English_____

2. _____

3. _____

4. _____

5. _____

After you've written your phrases, say them each seven times out loud, picturing them in your mind.

The Fun Page

Learn the colors!

Write down 10 colors.

Foreign Language	English
1._____	1._____
2._____	2._____
3._____	3._____
4._____	4._____
5._____	5._____
6._____	6._____
7._____	7._____
8._____	8._____
9._____	9._____
10._____	10._____

After you've written your words, say them each seven times out loud, picturing them in your mind.

Illustrate what you've learned.

Make Your Own Comic

Using inspiration from the previous pages, make your own comic in your new language.

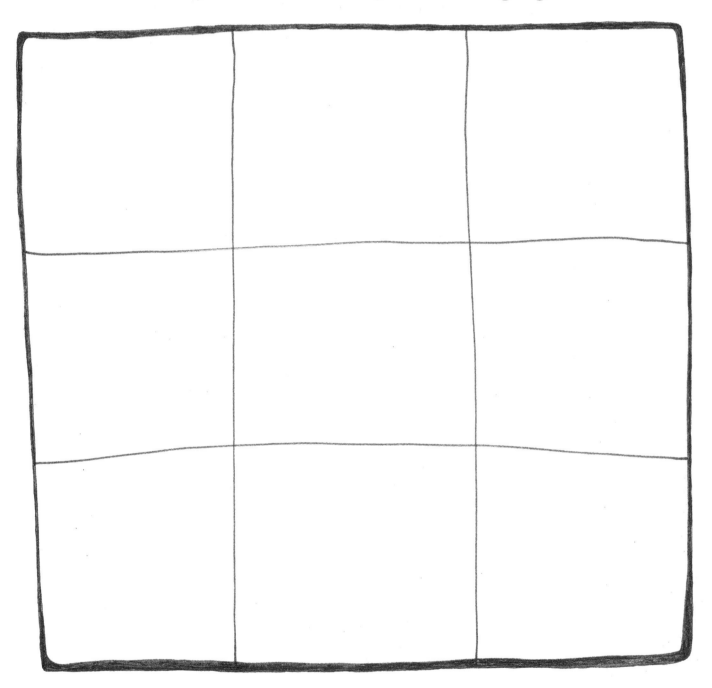

After you've finished, read your comic aloud seven times.

Add Words to the Doodle

**Find words to describe this picture.
Add your words to this page in a creative way.**

MOVIE TIME!

Watch a film, documentary, or YouTube video in your new language

Title: ....
....
Producer: ....
....
Actors: ....
....
....

10 WORDS

Write down 10 words you hear while watching the film.

Foreign Language	English
1. _____	1. _____
2. _____	2. _____
3. _____	3. _____
4. _____	4. _____
5. _____	5. _____
6. _____	6. _____
7. _____	7. _____
8. _____	8. _____
9. _____	9. _____
10. _____	10. _____

RATING:

- The Best
- Amazing
- Great
- Good
- Nice
- Ok
- Bad
- Horrible
- The Worst

HUMAN BODY
10 NEW WORDS!

Use a book, video, or Google Translate to find your ten words.

Foreign Language   **English**

_____   _____

_____   _____

_____   _____

_____   _____

_____   _____

_____   _____

_____   _____

_____   _____

_____   _____

_____   _____

Research ten words you might use in a conversation about the human body.

After written your words, say them each seven times out loud, picturing them in your mind.

Research Time!

FIVE NEW PHRASES!

Research five phrases you might use in a conversation about the human body.

1. _Foreign Language_
   English

2.

3.

4.

5.

After you've written your phrases, say them each seven times out loud, picturing them in your mind.

The Fun Page

ILLNESS

Make a list of ten common illnesses.

Foreign Language	English
1. _____	1. _____
2. _____	2. _____
3. _____	3. _____
4. _____	4. _____
5. _____	5. _____
6. _____	6. _____
7. _____	7. _____
8. _____	8. _____
9. _____	9. _____
10. _____	10. _____

After you've written your words, say them each seven times out loud, picturing them in your mind.

Illustrate what you've learned.

Add Words to the Doodle

Find words to describe this picture.
Add your words to this page in a creative way.

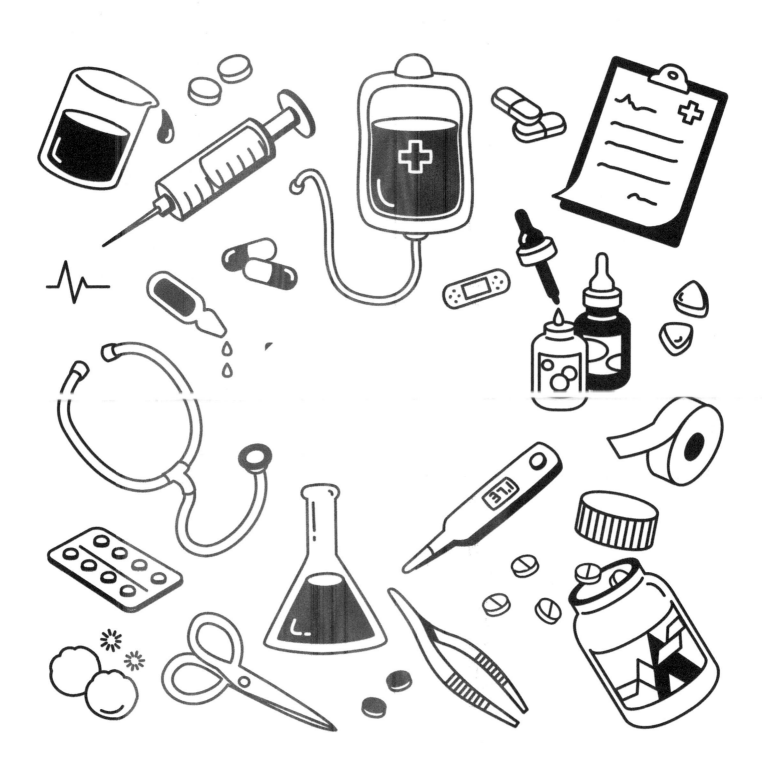

Make Your Own Texts

Using inspiration from the previous pages, make your own text conversation in your new language.

After you've finished, read your conversation aloud seven times.

MOVIE TIME!

Watch a film, documentary, or YouTube video in your new language

Title: ....
....
Producer: ....
....
Actors: ....
....
....

10 WORDS

Write down 10 words you hear while watching the film.

Foreign Language

1. _____
2. _____
3. _____
4. _____
5. _____
6. _____
7. _____
8. _____
9. _____
10. _____

English

1. _____
2. _____
3. _____
4. _____
5. _____
6. _____
7. _____
8. _____
9. _____
10. _____

RATING:

The Best

Amazing

Great

Good

Nice

Ok

Bad

Horrible

The Worst

THE HOLIDAYS
10 NEW WORDS!

Use a book, video, or Google Translate to find your ten words.

Foreign Language **English**

_____ _____
_____ _____
_____ _____
_____ _____
_____ _____
_____ _____
_____ _____
_____ _____
_____ _____
_____ _____

Research ten words you might use in a conversation about the holidays.

After written your words, say them each seven times out loud, picturing them in your mind.

Research Time!

FIVE NEW PHRASES!

Research five phrases you might use in a conversation about the holidays.

1. _Foreign Language_ _____

   English _____

2. _____

3. _____

4. _____

5. _____

After you've written your phrases, say them each seven times out loud, picturing them in your mind.

The Fun Page

The five most important sentences.
What do you think they are?

1. Foreign Language
   English

2. _____

3. _____

4. _____

5. _____

After you've written these sentences, say them each seven times out loud, picturing them in your mind.

Illustrate what you've learned.

Make Your Own Comic

Using inspiration from the previous pages, make your own comic in your new language.

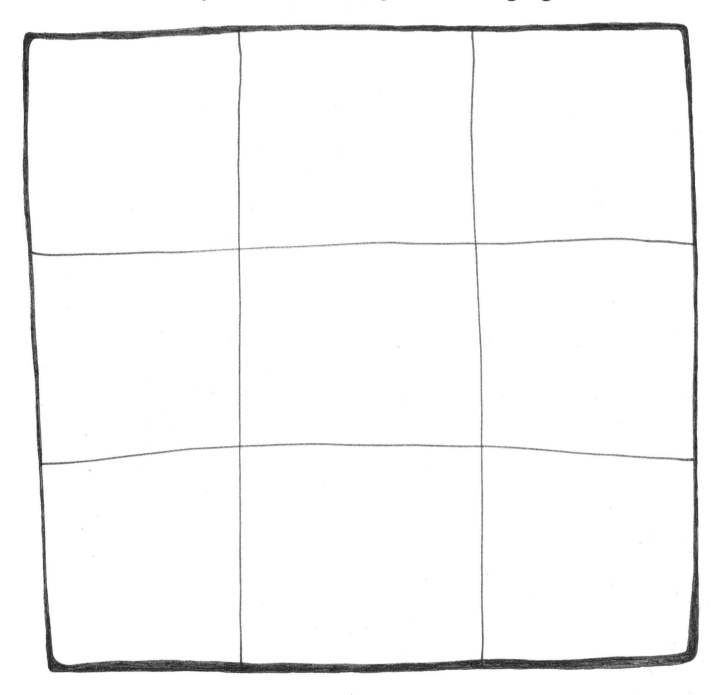

After you've finished, read your comic aloud seven times.

Add Words to the Doodle

**Find words to describe this picture.
Add your words to this page in a creative way.**

MOVIE TIME!

Watch a film, documentary, or YouTube video in your new language

Title: ....

Producer: ....

Actors: ....

10 WORDS

Write down 10 words you hear while watching the film.

Foreign Language

1. _____
2. _____
3. _____
4. _____
5. _____
6. _____
7. _____
8. _____
9. _____
10. _____

English

1. _____
2. _____
3. _____
4. _____
5. _____
6. _____
7. _____
8. _____
9. _____
10. _____

RATING:

The Best

Amazing

Great

Good

Nice

Ok

Bad

Horrible

The Worst

MUSIC
10 NEW WORDS!

Use a book, video, or Google Translate to find your ten words.

Foreign Language	English
_____	_____
_____	_____
_____	_____
_____	_____
_____	_____
_____	_____
_____	_____
_____	_____
_____	_____
_____	_____

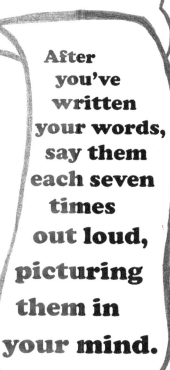

Research ten words you might use in a conversation about music.

After you've written your words, say them each seven times out loud, picturing them in your mind.

Research Time!

FIVE NEW PHRASES!

Research five phrases you might use in a conversation about music.

1. _Foreign Language_ _____
   English _____

2. _____

3. _____

4. _____

5. _____

After you've written your phrases, say them each seven times out loud, picturing them in your mind.

The Fun Page

Memorize a verse of a song in _____,

SONG TITLE:_____

_____
_____
_____
_____
_____
_____
_____
_____
_____
_____
_____
_____
_____
_____

After you've written these sentences, say them each seven times out loud, picturing them in your mind.

Illustrate what you've learned.

Add Words to the Doodle

**Find words to describe this picture.
Add your words to this page in a creative way.**

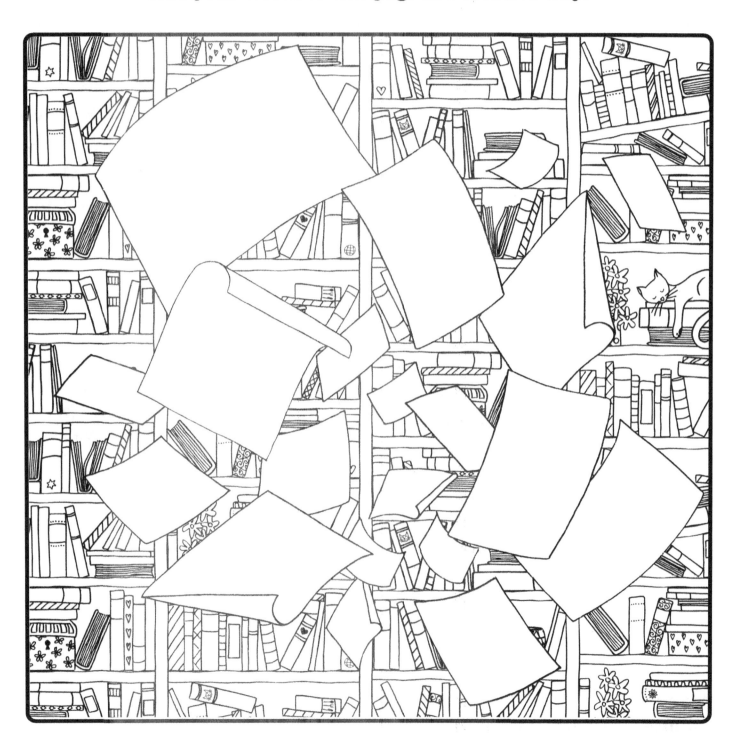

Make Your Own Texts

Using inspiration from the previous pages, make your own text conversation in _____ .

After you've finished, read your conversation aloud seven times.

MOVIE TIME!

Watch a film, documentary, or YouTube video in your new language

Title: ....
Producer: ....
Actors: ....

10 WORDS

Write down 10 words you hear while watching the film.

Foreign Language
1. _____
2. _____
3. _____
4. _____
5. _____
6. _____
7. _____
8. _____
9. _____
10. _____

English
1. _____
2. _____
3. _____
4. _____
5. _____
6. _____
7. _____
8. _____
9. _____
10. _____

RATING:

The Best

Amazing

Great

Good

Nice

Ok

Bad

Horrible

The Worst

DIRECTIONS
10 NEW WORDS!

Use a book, video, or Google Translate to find your ten words.

Foreign Language   **English**

_____   _____
_____   _____
_____   _____
_____   _____
_____   _____
_____   _____
_____   _____
_____   _____
_____   _____
_____   _____

Research ten words you might use in a conversation about directions.

After you've written your words, say them each seven times out loud, picturing them in your mind.

Research Time!

FIVE NEW PHRASES!

Research five phrases you might use in a conversation about directions.

1. _Foreign Language_
   English

2.

3.

4.

5.

After you've written your phrases, say them each seven times out loud, picturing them in your mind.

The Fun Page

INSULTS

Make a list in _____ of things you should never say!

1. <u>Foreign Language</u>
   <u> English </u>

2. _____

3. _____

4. _____

5. _____

After you've written these sentences, say them each seven times out loud, picturing them in your mind.

Illustrate what you've learned.

Add Words to the Doodle

**Find words to describe this picture.
Add your words to this page in a creative way.**

Make Your Own Texts

Using inspiration from the previous pages, make your own text conversation in your new language.

After you've finished, read your conversation aloud seven times.

MOVIE TIME!

Watch a film, documentary, or YouTube video in your new language

Title: ....
....
Producer: ....
....
Actors: ....
....
....

10 WORDS

Write down 10 words you hear while watching the film.

Foreign Language

1. _____
2. _____
3. _____
4. _____
5. _____
6. _____
7. _____
8. _____
9. _____
10. _____

English

1. _____
2. _____
3. _____
4. _____
5. _____
6. _____
7. _____
8. _____
9. _____
10. _____

RATING:

The Best

Amazing

Great

Good

Nice

Ok

Bad

Horrible

The Worst

FAMILY
10 NEW WORDS!

Use a book, video, or Google Translate to find your ten words.

Foreign Language   **English**

_____ _____

_____ _____

_____ _____

_____ _____

_____ _____

_____ _____

_____ _____

_____ _____

_____ _____

_____ _____

Research ten words you might use in a conversation about family.

After you've written your words, say them each seven times out loud, picturing them in your mind.

Research Time!

FIVE NEW PHRASES!

Research five phrases you might use in a conversation about family.

1. _Foreign Language_____

_____English_____

_____

2. _____

_____

_____

3. _____

_____

_____

4. _____

_____

_____

5. _____

_____

After you've written your phrases, say them each seven times out loud, picturing them in your mind.

The Fun Page

EMOTIONAL TALK: Shame

Write down five phrases you might use when ashamed.

1. Foreign Language _____
   English _____

2. _____
   _____

3. _____
   _____

4. _____
   _____

5. _____
   _____

After you've written these sentences, say them each seven times out loud, picturing them in your mind.

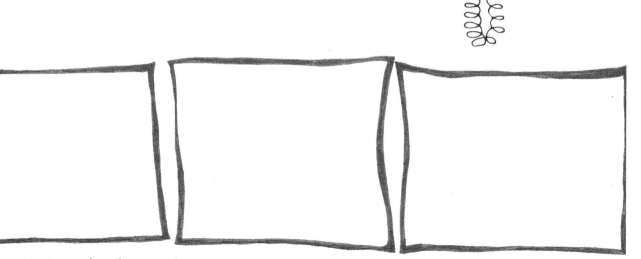

Illustrate what you've learned.

Make Your Own Comic

Using inspiration from the previous pages, make your own comic in _____ .

After you've finished, read your comic aloud seven times.

Make Your Own Texts

Using inspiration from the previous pages, make your own text conversation in _____ .

After you've finished, read your conversation aloud seven times.

MOVIE TIME!

Watch a film, documentary, or YouTube video in your new language

Title: ....
....
Producer: ....
....
Actors: ....
....
....

10 WORDS

Write down 10 words you hear while watching the film.

Foreign Language

1. _____
2. _____
3. _____
4. _____
5. _____
6. _____
7. _____
8. _____
9. _____
10. _____

English

1. _____
2. _____
3. _____
4. _____
5. _____
6. _____
7. _____
8. _____
9. _____
10. _____

RATING:

The Best

Amazing

Great

Good

Nice

Ok

Bad

Horrible

The Worst

CLOTHING
10 NEW WORDS!

Use a book, video, or Google Translate to find your ten words.

Foreign Language **English**

_____ _____
_____ _____
_____ _____
_____ _____
_____ _____
_____ _____
_____ _____
_____ _____
_____ _____
_____ _____

Research ten words you might use in a conversation about clothing.

After you've written your words, say them each seven times out loud, picturing them in your mind.

Research Time!

FIVE NEW PHRASES!

Research five phrases you might use in a conversation about clothing.

1. _Foreign Language_____
   _English_____
   _____

2. _____
   _____
   _____

3. _____
   _____
   _____

4. _____
   _____
   _____

5. _____
   _____

After you've written your phrases, say them each seven times out loud, picturing them in your mind.

The Fun Page

Research and translate slang from the _____ language.

1. __Foreign Language_____
   __English_____

2. _____
   _____

3. _____
   _____

4. _____
   _____

5. _____
   _____

After you've written these sentences, say them each seven times out loud, picturing them in your mind.

Illustrate what you've learned.

Make Your Own Comic

Using inspiration from the previous pages, make your own comic in _____ .

After you've finished, read your comic aloud seven times.

Add Words to the Doodle

**Find words to describe this picture.
Add your words to this page in a creative way.**

MOVIE TIME!

Watch a film, documentary, or YouTube video in your new language

Title: ....
....
Producer: ....
....
Actors: ....
....
....

10 WORDS

Write down 10 words you hear while watching the film.

Foreign Language   English

1. _____   1. _____
2. _____   2. _____
3. _____   3. _____
4. _____   4. _____
5. _____   5. _____
6. _____   6. _____
7. _____   7. _____
8. _____   8. _____
9. _____   9. _____
10. _____   10. _____

RATING:

The Best

Amazing

Great

Good

Nice

Ok

Bad

Horrible

The Worst

ENTERTAINMENT
10 NEW WORDS!

Use a book, video, or Google Translate to find your ten words.

Foreign Language	English
_____	_____
_____	_____
_____	_____
_____	_____
_____	_____
_____	_____
_____	_____
_____	_____
_____	_____
_____	_____

Research ten words you might use in a conversation about entertainment.

After you've written your words, say them each seven times out loud, picturing them in your mind.

Research Time!

FIVE NEW PHRASES!

Research five phrases you might use in a conversation about entertainment.

1. _Foreign Language_____
   _English_____

2. _____
   _____

3. _____
   _____

4. _____
   _____

5. _____
   _____

After you've written your phrases, say them each seven times out loud, picturing them in your mind.

The Fun Page

SORRY!

How many different ways can you say you're sorry?

1. Foreign Language _____
   English _____

2. _____
   _____

3. _____
   _____

4. _____
   _____

5. _____
   _____

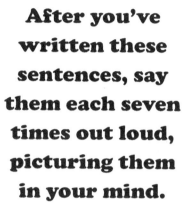

After you've written these sentences, say them each seven times out loud, picturing them in your mind.

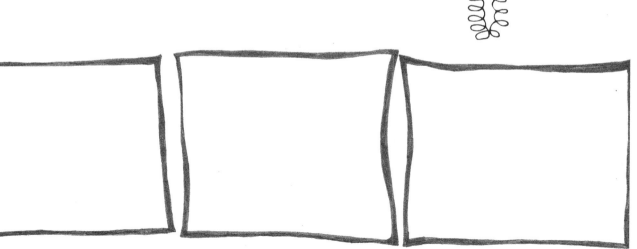

Illustrate what you've learned.

Add Words to the Doodle

**Find words to describe this picture.
Add your words to this page in a creative way.**

Make Your Own Texts

Using inspiration from the previous pages, make your own text conversation in _____ .

After you've finished, read your conversation aloud seven times.

MOVIE TIME!

Watch a film, documentary, or YouTube video in your new language

Title: ....
....
Producer: ....
....
Actors: ....
....
....

10 WORDS

Write down 10 words you hear while watching the film.

Foreign Language

1. _____
2. _____
3. _____
4. _____
5. _____
6. _____
7. _____
8. _____
9. _____
10. _____

English

1. _____
2. _____
3. _____
4. _____
5. _____
6. _____
7. _____
8. _____
9. _____
10. _____

RATING:

The Best

Amazing

Great

Good

Nice

Ok

Bad

Horrible

The Worst

EMOTIONS
10 NEW WORDS!

Use a book, video, or Google Translate to find your ten words.

Foreign Language　　　　　**English**

_____　　_____

_____　　_____

_____　　_____

_____　　_____

_____　　_____

_____　　_____

_____　　_____

_____　　_____

_____　　_____

_____　　_____

Research ten words you might use in a conversation about emotions.

After you've written your words, say them each seven times out loud, picturing them in your mind.

Research Time!

FIVE NEW PHRASES!

Research five phrases you might use in a conversation about emotions.

1. __Foreign Language_____

   __English_____

2. _____
   _____

3. _____
   _____

4. _____
   _____

5. _____
   _____

After you've written your phrases, say them each seven times out loud, picturing them in your mind.

The Fun Page

EMOTIONAL TALK: Sadness
Write down ten words that make you sad.

Foreign Language	English
1._____	1._____
2._____	2._____
3._____	3._____
4._____	4._____
5._____	5._____
6._____	6._____
7._____	7._____
8._____	8._____
9._____	9._____
10._____	10._____

After you've written your words, say them each seven times out loud, picturing them in your mind.

Illustrate what you've learned.

Make Your Own Comic

Using inspiration from the previous pages, make your own comic in _____ .

After you've finished, read your comic aloud seven times.

Make Your Own Texts

Using inspiration from the previous pages, make your own text conversation in _____.

After you've finished, read your conversation aloud seven times.

MOVIE TIME!

Watch a film, documentary, or YouTube video in your new language

Title: ....
....
Producer: ....
....
Actors: ....
....
....

10 WORDS

Write down 10 words you hear while watching the film.

Foreign Language

1. _____
2. _____
3. _____
4. _____
5. _____
6. _____
7. _____
8. _____
9. _____
10. _____

English

1. _____
2. _____
3. _____
4. _____
5. _____
6. _____
7. _____
8. _____
9. _____
10. _____

RATING:

The Best

Amazing

Great

Good

Nice

Ok

Bad

Horrible

The Worst

POLITICS
10 NEW WORDS!

Use a book, video, or Google Translate to find your ten words.

Foreign Language   **English**

_____ _____

_____ _____

_____ _____

_____ _____

_____ _____

_____ _____

_____ _____

_____ _____

_____ _____

_____ _____

Research ten words you might use in a conversation about politics.

After you've written your words, say them each seven times out loud, picturing them in your mind.

Research Time!

FIVE NEW PHRASES!

Research five phrases you might use in a conversation about politics.

1. ___Foreign Language_____

___English_____

_____

2. _____

_____

_____

3. _____

_____

_____

4. _____

_____

_____

5. _____

_____

After you've written your phrases, say them each seven times out loud, picturing them in your mind.

The Fun Page

Write ten things you love.

After you've written your words, say them each seven times out loud, picturing them in your mind.

Foreign Language	English
1._____	1._____
2._____	2._____
3._____	3._____
4._____	4._____
5._____	5._____
6._____	6._____
7._____	7._____
8._____	8._____
9._____	9._____
10._____	10._____

Illustrate what you've learned.

Make Your Own Comic

Using inspiration from the previous pages, make your own comic in your new language.

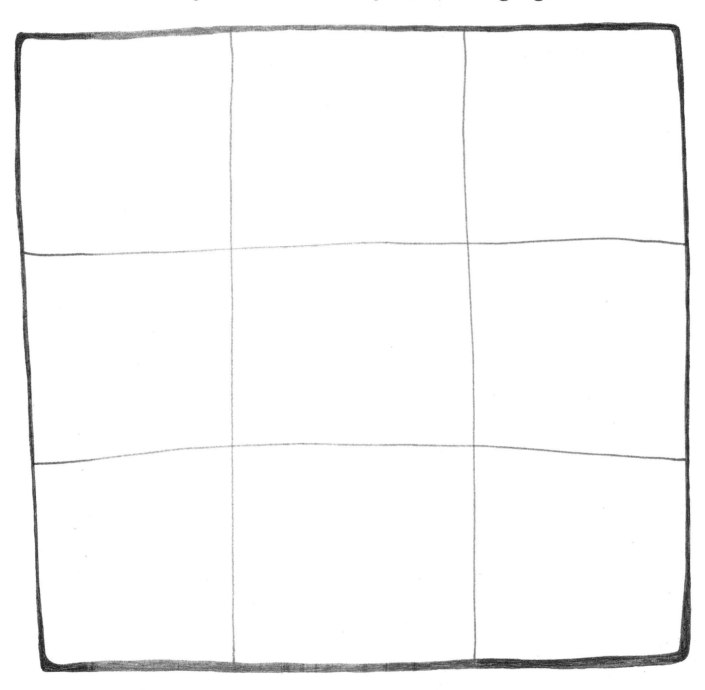

After you've finished, read your comic aloud seven times.

Add Words to the Doodle

**Find words to describe this picture.
Add your words to this page in a creative way.**

MOVIE TIME!

Watch a film, documentary, or YouTube video in your new language

Title: ....
....
Producer: ....
....
Actors: ....
....
....

10 WORDS

Write down 10 words you hear while watching the film.

Foreign Language

1. _____
2. _____
3. _____
4. _____
5. _____
6. _____
7. _____
8. _____
9. _____
10. _____

English

1. _____
2. _____
3. _____
4. _____
5. _____
6. _____
7. _____
8. _____
9. _____
10. _____

RATING:

The Best

Amazing

Great

Good

Nice

Ok

Bad

Horrible

The Worst

SOCIETY
10 NEW WORDS!

Use a book, video, or Google Translate to find your ten words.

Foreign Language　　　　**English**

_____　　_____

_____　　_____

_____　　_____

_____　　_____

_____　　_____

_____　　_____

_____　　_____

_____　　_____

_____　　_____

_____　　_____

Research ten words you might use in a conversation about society.

After you've written your words, say them each seven times out loud, picturing them in your mind.

Research Time!

FIVE NEW PHRASES!

Research five phrases you might use in a conversation about society.

1. __Foreign Language_____
   __English_____

2. _____
   _____

3. _____
   _____

4. _____
   _____

5. _____
   _____

After you've written your phrases, say them each seven times out loud, picturing them in your mind.

The Fun Page

Research three common jokes in your new language, with the translation.
(Jokes often don't translate well!)

1. _____
_____
_____
_____

After you've written these sentences, say them each seven times out loud, picturing them in your mind.

2. _____
_____
_____
_____
_____

3. _____
_____
_____
_____
_____

Illustrate what you've learned.

Make Your Own Comic

Using inspiration from the previous pages, make your own comic in _____ .

After you've finished, read your comic aloud seven times.

Make Your Own Texts

Using inspiration from the previous pages, make your own text conversation in _____ .

After you've finished, read your conversation aloud seven times.

MOVIE TIME!

Watch a film, documentary, or YouTube video in your new language

Title: ....
....
Producer: ....
....
Actors: ....
....
....

10 WORDS

Write down 10 words you hear while watching the film.

Foreign Language

1. _____
2. _____
3. _____
4. _____
5. _____
6. _____
7. _____
8. _____
9. _____
10. _____

English

1. _____
2. _____
3. _____
4. _____
5. _____
6. _____
7. _____
8. _____
9. _____
10. _____

RATING:

The Best

Amazing

Great

Good

Nice

Ok

Bad

Horrible

The Worst

RELIGION
10 NEW WORDS!

Use a book, video, or Google Translate to find your ten words.

Foreign Language	English
_____	_____
_____	_____
_____	_____
_____	_____
_____	_____
_____	_____
_____	_____
_____	_____
_____	_____
_____	_____

Research ten words you might use in a conversation about religion.

After you've written your words, say them each seven times out loud, picturing them in your mind.

Research Time!

FIVE NEW PHRASES!

Research five phrases you might use in a conversation about religion.

1. __Foreign Language_____

   __English_____

2. _____

3. _____

4. _____

5. _____

After you've written your phrases, say them each seven times out loud, picturing them in your mind.

The Fun Page

Find a recipe from a place where the language you're studying originated. Translate the recipe and Copy it down here.

What's cooking? _____

Instructions Below:
_____
_____
_____
_____
_____
_____
_____
_____
_____
_____
_____
_____
_____
_____

After you've written the recipe, read it aloud seven times, picturing the words in your mind.

Illustrate what you've learned.

Make Your Own Comic

Using inspiration from the previous pages, make your own comic in your new language.

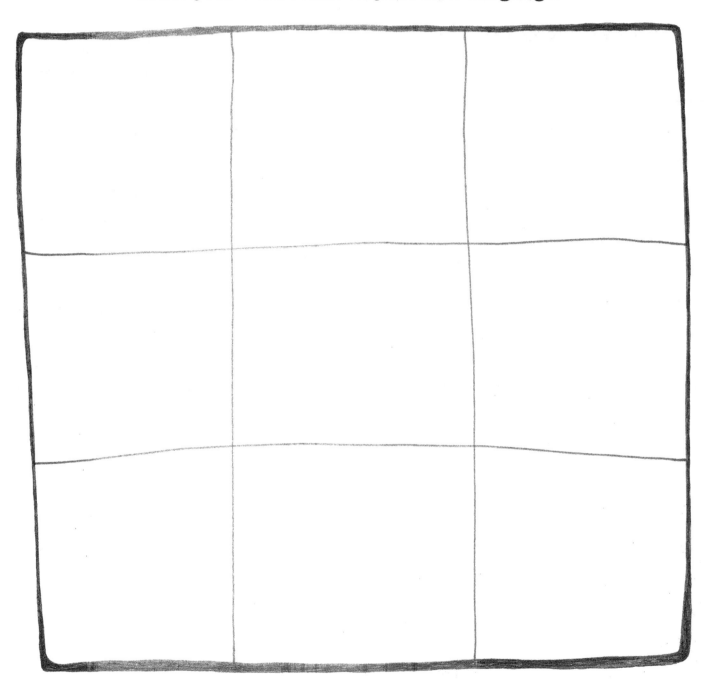

After you've finished, read your comic aloud seven times.

Add Words to the Doodle

**Find words to describe this picture.
Add your words to this page in a creative way.**

MOVIE TIME!

Watch a film, documentary, or YouTube video in your new language

Title: ....
....
Producer: ....
....
Actors: ....
....
....

10 WORDS

Write down 10 words you hear while watching the film.

Foreign Language	English
1. _____	1. _____
2. _____	2. _____
3. _____	3. _____
4. _____	4. _____
5. _____	5. _____
6. _____	6. _____
7. _____	7. _____
8. _____	8. _____
9. _____	9. _____
10. _____	10. _____

RATING:

The Best

Amazing

Great

Good

Nice

Ok

Bad

Horrible

The Worst

Coffee & Tea
10 NEW WORDS!

Use a book, video, or Google Translate to find your ten words.

Foreign Language **English**

_____ _____
_____ _____
_____ _____
_____ _____
_____ _____
_____ _____
_____ _____
_____ _____
_____ _____
_____ _____

Research ten words you might use in a conversation about coffee and tea.

After you've written your words, say them each seven times out loud, picturing them in your mind.

Research Time!

FIVE NEW PHRASES!

Research five phrases you might use in a conversation about coffee and tea.

1. _Foreign Language_____
   _English_____

2. _____

3. _____

4. _____

5. _____

After you've written your phrases, say them each seven times out loud, picturing them in your mind.

The Fun Page

Make a list in _____ of ten different occupations.

Foreign Language	English
1._____	1._____
2._____	2._____
3._____	3._____
4._____	4._____
5._____	5._____
6._____	6._____
7._____	7._____
8._____	8._____
9._____	9._____
10._____	10._____

After you've written your words, say them each seven times out loud, picturing them in your mind.

Illustrate what you've learned.

Add Words to the Doodle

**Find words to describe this picture.
Add your words to this page in a creative way.**

Make Your Own Texts

Using inspiration from the previous pages,
make your own text conversation in _____ .

After you've finished, read your conversation aloud seven times.

MOVIE TIME!

Watch a film, documentary, or YouTube video in your new language

Title: ....
....
Producer: ....
....
Actors: ....
....
....

10 WORDS

Write down 10 words you hear while watching the film.

Foreign Language

1. _____
2. _____
3. _____
4. _____
5. _____
6. _____
7. _____
8. _____
9. _____
10. _____

English

1. _____
2. _____
3. _____
4. _____
5. _____
6. _____
7. _____
8. _____
9. _____
10. _____

RATING:

The Best

Amazing

Great

Good

Nice

Ok

Bad

Horrible

The Worst

The Arts
10 NEW WORDS!

> Use a book, video, or Google Translate to find your ten words.

Foreign Language	English
_____	_____
_____	_____
_____	_____
_____	_____
_____	_____
_____	_____
_____	_____
_____	_____
_____	_____
_____	_____

Research ten words you might use in a conversation about the arts.

> After you've written your words, say them each seven times out loud, picturing them in your mind.

Research Time!

FIVE NEW PHRASES!

Research five phrases you might use in a conversation about the arts

1. _Foreign Language_ _____
   English _____

2. _____

3. _____

4. _____

5. _____

After you've written your phrases, say them each seven times out loud, picturing them in your mind.

The Fun Page

More compliments!
Be creative! Translate five compliments and then practice using them.

1. Foreign Language
   English

2.

3.

4.

5.

After you've written these sentences, say them each seven times out loud, picturing them in your mind.

Illustrate what you've learned.

Add Words to the Doodle

**Find words to describe this picture.
Add your words to this page in a creative way.**

Make Your Own Texts

**Using inspiration from the previous pages,
make your own text conversation in your new language.**

After you've finished, read your conversation aloud seven times.

MOVIE TIME!

Watch a film, documentary, or YouTube video in your new language

Title: ....
....
Producer: ....
....
Actors: ....
....
....

10 WORDS

Write down 10 words you hear while watching the film.

Foreign Language	English
1._____	1._____
2._____	2._____
3._____	3._____
4._____	4._____
5._____	5._____
6._____	6._____
7._____	7._____
8._____	8._____
9._____	9._____
10._____	10._____

RATING:

The Best

Amazing

Great

Good

Nice

Ok

Bad

Horrible

The Worst

HOME
10 NEW WORDS!

Use a book, video, or Google Translate to find your ten words.

Foreign Language   **English**

_____   _____

_____   _____

_____   _____

_____   _____

_____   _____

_____   _____

_____   _____

_____   _____

_____   _____

_____   _____

Research ten words you might use in a conversation about home.

After you've written your words, say them each seven times out loud, picturing them in your mind.

Research Time!

FIVE NEW PHRASES!

Research five phrases you might use in a conversation about home.

1. <u>Foreign Language</u>

   <u>English</u>

2. _____

3. _____

4. _____

5. _____

After you've written your phrases, say them each seven times out loud, picturing them in your mind.

The Fun Page

Hello!

How many ways can you say hello?

Foreign Language	English
1._____	1._____
2._____	2._____
3._____	3._____
4._____	4._____
5._____	5._____
6._____	6._____
7._____	7._____
8._____	8._____
9._____	9._____
10._____	10._____

After you've written your words, say them each seven times out loud, picturing them in your mind.

Illustrate what you've learned.

Add Words to the Doodle

**Find words to describe this picture.
Add your words to this page in a creative way.**

Make Your Own Texts

Using inspiration from the previous pages, make your own text conversation in _____ .

After you've finished, read your conversation aloud seven times.

MOVIE TIME!

Watch a film, documentary, or YouTube video in your new language

Title: ....
....
Producer: ....
....
Actors: ....
....
....

10 WORDS

Write down 10 words you hear while watching the film.

Foreign Language

1. _____
2. _____
3. _____
4. _____
5. _____
6. _____
7. _____
8. _____
9. _____
10. _____

English

1. _____
2. _____
3. _____
4. _____
5. _____
6. _____
7. _____
8. _____
9. _____
10. _____

RATING:

The Best

Amazing

Great

Good

Nice

Ok

Bad

Horrible

The Worst

ELECTRONICS
10 NEW WORDS!

Use a book, video, or Google Translate to find your ten words.

Foreign Language	English
_____	_____
_____	_____
_____	_____
_____	_____
_____	_____
_____	_____
_____	_____
_____	_____
_____	_____
_____	_____

Research ten words you might use in a conversation about electronics.

After you've written your words, say them each seven times out loud, picturing them in your mind.

Research Time!

FIVE NEW PHRASES!

Research five phrases you might use in a conversation about electronics.

1. _Foreign Language_ _____

   English _____

   _____

2. _____

   _____

   _____

3. _____

   _____

   _____

4. _____

   _____

   _____

5. _____

   _____

After you've written your phrases, say them each seven times out loud, picturing them in your mind.

The Fun Page

EMOTIONAL TALK: Anger

Write down ten angry words and their translations.

Foreign Language	English
1._____	1._____
2._____	2._____
3._____	3._____
4._____	4._____
5._____	5._____
6._____	6._____
7._____	7._____
8._____	8._____
9._____	9._____
10._____	10._____

After you've written your words, say them each seven times out loud, picturing them in your mind.

Illustrate what you've learned.

Make Your Own Comic

Using inspiration from the previous pages, make your own comic in your new language.

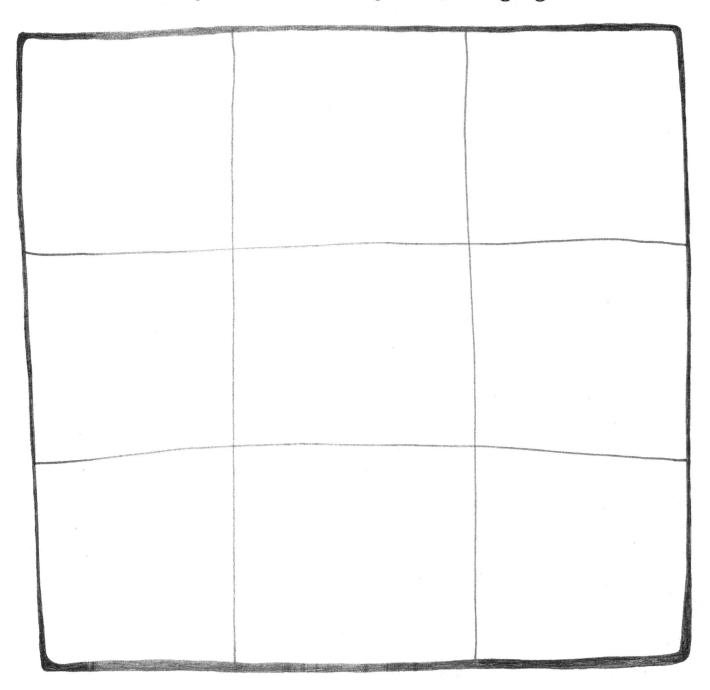

After you've finished, read your comic aloud seven times.

Add Words to the Doodle

**Find words to describe this picture.
Add your words to this page in a creative way.**

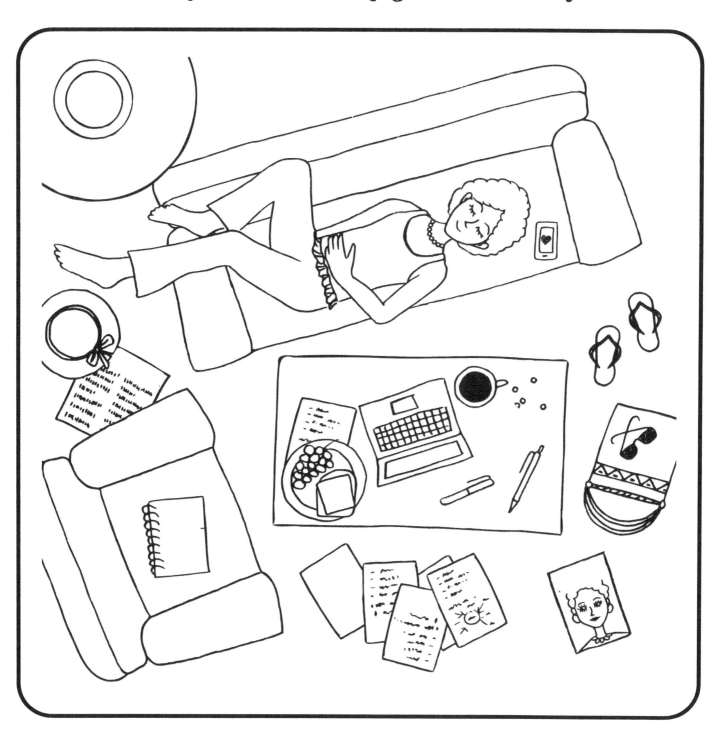

MOVIE TIME!

Watch a film, documentary, or YouTube video in your new language

Title: ....
....
Producer: ....
....
Actors: ....
....
....

10 WORDS

Write down 10 words you hear while watching the film.

Foreign Language

1. _____
2. _____
3. _____
4. _____
5. _____
6. _____
7. _____
8. _____
9. _____
10. _____

English

1. _____
2. _____
3. _____
4. _____
5. _____
6. _____
7. _____
8. _____
9. _____
10. _____

RATING:

The Best

Amazing

Great

Good

Nice

Ok

Bad

Horrible

The Worst

Restaurants
10 NEW WORDS!

Use a book, video, or Google Translate to find your ten words.

Foreign Language　　　　　**English**

_____　_____

_____　_____

_____　_____

_____　_____

_____　_____

_____　_____

_____　_____

_____　_____

_____　_____

_____　_____

Research ten words you might use in a conversation about restaurants.

After you've written your words, say them each seven times out loud, picturing them in your mind.

Research Time!

FIVE NEW PHRASES!

Research five phrases you might use in a conversation about restaurants.

1. Foreign Language _____
   English _____

2. _____
   _____

3. _____
   _____

4. _____
   _____

5. _____
   _____

After you've written your phrases, say them each seven times out loud, picturing them in your mind.

The Fun Page

Write a short story in your new language.

After you've written the story, read it seven times out loud, picturing each word in your mind.

Illustrate what you've learned.

Add Words to the Doodle

**Find words to describe this picture.
Add your words to this page in a creative way.**

Make Your Own Texts

Using inspiration from the previous pages, make your own text conversation in _____ .

After you've finished, read your conversation aloud seven times.

MOVIE TIME!

Watch a film, documentary, or YouTube video in your new language

Title: ....
....
Producer: ....
....
Actors: ....
....
....

10 WORDS

Write down 10 words you hear while watching the film.

Foreign Language

1. _____
2. _____
3. _____
4. _____
5. _____
6. _____
7. _____
8. _____
9. _____
10. _____

English

1. _____
2. _____
3. _____
4. _____
5. _____
6. _____
7. _____
8. _____
9. _____
10. _____

RATING:

The Best

Amazing

Great

Good

Nice

Ok

Bad

Horrible

The Worst

DANCE
10 NEW WORDS!

Use a book, video, or Google Translate to find your ten words.

Foreign Language	English
_____	_____
_____	_____
_____	_____
_____	_____
_____	_____
_____	_____
_____	_____
_____	_____
_____	_____
_____	_____

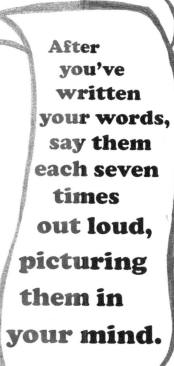

Research ten words you might use in a conversation about dancing.

After you've written your words, say them each seven times out loud, picturing them in your mind.

Research Time!

FIVE NEW PHRASES!

Research five phrases you might use in a conversation about dancing.

1. **Foreign Language** _____

   English _____

   _____

2. _____

   _____

   _____

3. _____

   _____

   _____

4. _____

   _____

   _____

5. _____

   _____

After you've written your phrases, say them each seven times out loud, picturing them in your mind.

The Fun Page

Watch a musical or dance performance from the country of your new language.

Write down ten words you hear while watching and translate them.

After you've written your words, say them each seven times out loud, picturing them in your mind.

Foreign Language	English
1._____	1._____
2._____	2._____
3._____	3._____
4._____	4._____
5._____	5._____
6._____	6._____
7._____	7._____
8._____	8._____
9._____	9._____
10._____	10._____

Illustrate what you've learned.

Make Your Own Comic

Using inspiration from the previous pages, make your own comic in your new language.

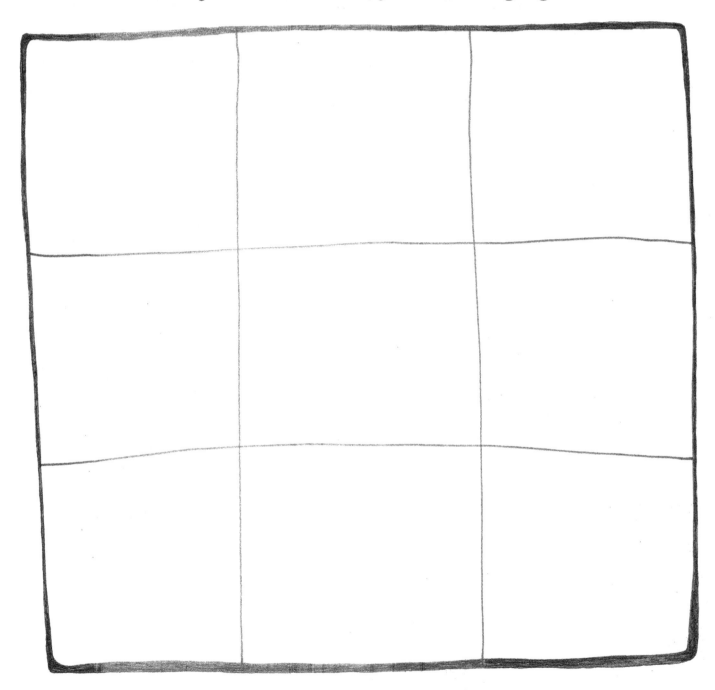

After you've finished, read your comic aloud seven times.

Add Words to the Doodle

**Find words to describe this picture.
Add your words to this page in a creative way.**

MOVIE TIME!

Watch a film, documentary, or YouTube video in your new language

Title: ....
....
Producer: ....
....
Actors: ....
....
....

10 WORDS

Write down 10 words you hear while watching the film.

Foreign Language

1. _____
2. _____
3. _____
4. _____
5. _____
6. _____
7. _____
8. _____
9. _____
10. _____

English

1. _____
2. _____
3. _____
4. _____
5. _____
6. _____
7. _____
8. _____
9. _____
10. _____

RATING:

The Best

Amazing

Great

Good

Nice

Ok

Bad

Horrible

The Worst

NATURE
10 NEW WORDS!

Use a book, video, or Google Translate to find your ten words.

Foreign Language	English
_____	_____
_____	_____
_____	_____
_____	_____
_____	_____
_____	_____
_____	_____
_____	_____
_____	_____
_____	_____

Research ten words you might use in a conversation about nature.

After you've written your words, say them each seven times out loud, picturing them in your mind.

Research Time!

FIVE NEW PHRASES!

Research five phrases you might use in a conversation about nature.

1. _Foreign Language_ _____

___ _English_ _____

_____

2. _____

_____

_____

3. _____

_____

_____

4. _____

_____

_____

5. _____

_____

After you've written your phrases, say them each seven times out loud, picturing them in your mind.

The Fun Page

Copy a poem about nature in your new language.

_____
_____
_____
_____
_____
_____
_____
_____
_____
_____
_____
_____
_____
_____
_____

After you've written this poem, say it out loud seven times, picturing the words in your mind.

Illustrate what you've learned.

Make Your Own Comic

Using inspiration from the previous pages, make your own comic in your new language.

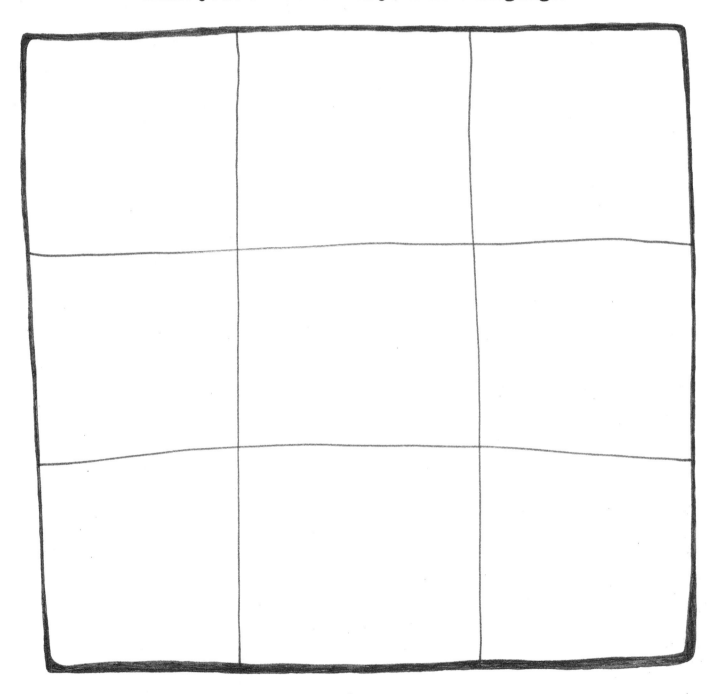

After you've finished, read your comic aloud seven times.

Add Words to the Doodle

**Find words to describe this picture.
Add your words to this page in a creative way.**

MOVIE TIME!

Watch a film, documentary, or YouTube video in your new language

Title: ....
....
Producer: ....
....
Actors: ....
....
....

10 WORDS

Write down 10 words you hear while watching the film.

Foreign Language

1. _____
2. _____
3. _____
4. _____
5. _____
6. _____
7. _____
8. _____
9. _____
10. _____

English

1. _____
2. _____
3. _____
4. _____
5. _____
6. _____
7. _____
8. _____
9. _____
10. _____

RATING:

The Best

Amazing

Great

Good

Nice

Ok

Bad

Horrible

The Worst

MATH/MEASUREMENTS
10 NEW WORDS!

Use a book, video, or Google Translate to find your ten words.

Foreign Language	English
_____	_____
_____	_____
_____	_____
_____	_____
_____	_____
_____	_____
_____	_____
_____	_____
_____	_____
_____	_____

Research ten words you might use in a conversation about math/measurements.

After you've written your words, say them each seven times out loud, picturing them in your mind.

Research Time!

FIVE NEW PHRASES!

Research five phrases you might use in a conversation about math/measurements.

1. _Foreign Language_____

   _English_____

2. _____
   _____

3. _____
   _____

4. _____
   _____

5. _____
   _____

After you've written your phrases, say them each seven times out loud, picturing them in your mind.

The Fun Page

Numbers & Counting

Practice counting and write the names of each number from one to ten.

Foreign Language	English
1._____	1._____
2._____	2._____
3._____	3._____
4._____	4._____
5._____	5._____
6._____	6._____
7._____	7._____
8._____	8._____
9._____	9._____
10._____	10._____

After you've written your words, say them each seven times out loud, picturing them in your mind.

Illustrate what you've learned.

Make Your Own Comic

Using inspiration from the previous pages,
make your own comic in _____ .

After you've finished, read your comic aloud seven times.

Add Words to the Doodle

**Find words to describe this picture.
Add your words to this page in a creative way.**

MOVIE TIME!

Watch a film, documentary, or YouTube video in your new language

Title: ....
....
Producer: ....
....
Actors: ....
....
....

10 WORDS

Write down 10 words you hear while watching the film.

Foreign Language

1. _____
2. _____
3. _____
4. _____
5. _____
6. _____
7. _____
8. _____
9. _____
10. _____

English

1. _____
2. _____
3. _____
4. _____
5. _____
6. _____
7. _____
8. _____
9. _____
10. _____

RATING:

The Best

Amazing

Great

Good

Nice

Ok

Bad

Horrible

The Worst

SEASONS
10 NEW WORDS!

Use a book, video, or Google Translate to find your ten words.

Foreign Language   **English**

_____ _____
_____ _____
_____ _____
_____ _____
_____ _____
_____ _____
_____ _____
_____ _____
_____ _____
_____ _____

Research ten words you might use in a conversation about seasons.

After you've written your words, say them each seven times out loud, picturing them in your mind.

Research Time!

FIVE NEW PHRASES!

Research five phrases you might use in a conversation about seasons.

1. _Foreign Language_

___English___

2.

3.

4.

5.

After you've written your phrases, say them each seven times out loud, picturing them in your mind.

The Fun Page

What are five sentences you use daily?

1. Foreign Language _____
   English _____

2. _____
   _____

3. _____
   _____

4. _____
   _____

5. _____
   _____

After you've written these sentences, say them each seven times out loud, picturing them in your mind.

Illustrate what you've learned.

Make Your Own Comic

Using inspiration from the previous pages, make your own comic in your new language.

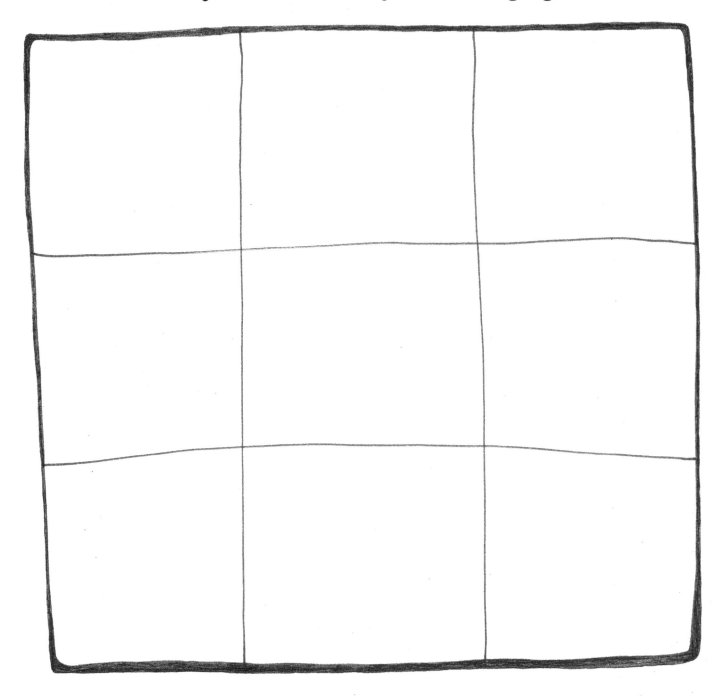

After you've finished, read your comic aloud seven times.

Add Words to the Doodle

**Find words to describe this picture.
Add your words to this page in a creative way.**

MOVIE TIME!

Watch a film, documentary, or YouTube video in your new language

Title: ....
....
Producer: ....
....
Actors: ....
....
....

10 WORDS

Write down 10 words you hear while watching the film.

Foreign Language

1. _____
2. _____
3. _____
4. _____
5. _____
6. _____
7. _____
8. _____
9. _____
10. _____

English

1. _____
2. _____
3. _____
4. _____
5. _____
6. _____
7. _____
8. _____
9. _____
10. _____

RATING:

The Best

Amazing

Great

Good

Nice

Ok

Bad

Horrible

The Worst

Weather
10 NEW WORDS!

Use a book, video, or Google Translate to find your ten words.

Foreign Language	English
_____	_____
_____	_____
_____	_____
_____	_____
_____	_____
_____	_____
_____	_____
_____	_____
_____	_____
_____	_____

Research ten words you might use in a conversation about weather.

After you've written your words, say them each seven times out loud, picturing them in your mind.

Research Time!

FIVE NEW PHRASES!

Research five phrases you might use in a conversation about weather.

1. _Foreign Language_____
   _English_____

2. _____
   _____

3. _____
   _____

4. _____
   _____

5. _____
   _____

After you've written your phrases, say them each seven times out loud, picturing them in your mind.

The Fun Page

EMOTIONAL TALK: Nervousness

Make a list of five phrases you might use when feeling nervous.

1. Foreign Language
   English

2.

3.

4.

5.

After you've written these sentences, say them each seven times out loud, picturing them in your mind.

Illustrate what you've learned.

Make Your Own Comic

Using inspiration from the previous pages, make your own comic in your new language.

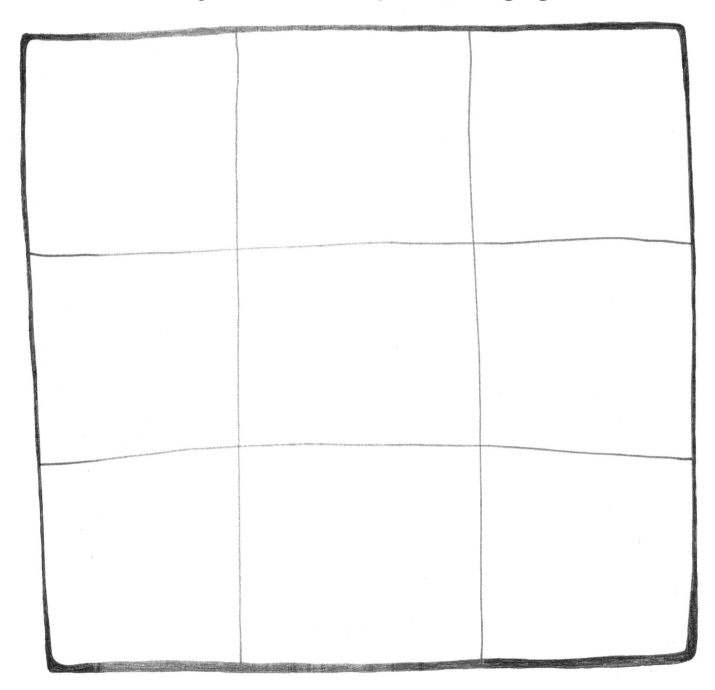

After you've finished, read your comic aloud seven times.

Make Your Own Texts

**Using inspiration from the previous pages,
make your own text conversation in your new language.**

After you've finished, read your conversation aloud seven times.

MOVIE TIME!

Watch a film, documentary, or YouTube video in your new language

Title: ....
....
Producer: ....
....
Actors: ....
....
....

10 WORDS

Write down 10 words you hear while watching the film.

Foreign Language

1. _____
2. _____
3. _____
4. _____
5. _____
6. _____
7. _____
8. _____
9. _____
10. _____

English

1. _____
2. _____
3. _____
4. _____
5. _____
6. _____
7. _____
8. _____
9. _____
10. _____

RATING:

The Best

Amazing

Great

Good

Nice

Ok

Bad

Horrible

The Worst

SHOPPING
10 NEW WORDS!

Use a book, video, or Google Translate to find your ten words.

Foreign Language **English**

_____ _____
_____ _____
_____ _____
_____ _____
_____ _____
_____ _____
_____ _____
_____ _____
_____ _____
_____ _____

Research ten words you might use in a conversation about shopping.

After you've written your words, say them each seven times out loud, picturing them in your mind.

Research Time!

FIVE NEW PHRASES!

Research five phrases you might use in a conversation about shopping.

1. __Foreign Language_____

   __English_____

   _____

2. _____

   _____

   _____

3. _____

   _____

   _____

4. _____

   _____

   _____

5. _____

   _____

After you've written your phrases, say them each seven times out loud, picturing them in your mind.

The Fun Page

Sayings and Quotes

Translate five common quotes or sayings.

1. **Foreign Language** _____
   English _____

2. _____
   _____

3. _____
   _____

4. _____
   _____

5. _____
   _____

After you've written these sentences, say them each seven times out loud, picturing them in your mind.

Illustrate what you've learned.

Make Your Own Comic

Using inspiration from the previous pages,
make your own comic in _____ .

After you've finished, read your comic aloud seven times.

Make Your Own Texts

Using inspiration from the previous pages, make your own text conversation in _____ .

After you've finished, read your conversation aloud seven times.

MOVIE TIME!

Watch a film, documentary, or YouTube video in your new language

Title: ....
....
Producer: ....
....
Actors: ....
....
....

10 WORDS

Write down 10 words you hear while watching the film.

Foreign Language	English
1. _____	1. _____
2. _____	2. _____
3. _____	3. _____
4. _____	4. _____
5. _____	5. _____
6. _____	6. _____
7. _____	7. _____
8. _____	8. _____
9. _____	9. _____
10. _____	10. _____

RATING:

The Best

Amazing

Great

Good

Nice

Ok

Bad

Horrible

The Worst

Date & Time
10 NEW WORDS!

Use a book, video, or Google Translate to find your ten words.

Foreign Language   **English**

_____ _____

_____ _____

_____ _____

_____ _____

_____ _____

_____ _____

_____ _____

_____ _____

_____ _____

_____ _____

Research ten words you might use in a conversation about time and date.

After you've written your words, say them each seven times out loud, picturing them in your mind.

Research Time!

FIVE NEW PHRASES!

Research five phrases you might use in a conversation about date and time

1. Foreign Language _____
   English _____

2. _____
   _____

3. _____
   _____

4. _____
   _____

5. _____
   _____

After you've written your phrases, say them each seven times out loud, picturing them in your mind.

The Fun Page

Color while you listen to music in your new language.

Illustrate what you've learned.

Make Your Own Comic

Using inspiration from the previous pages, make your own comic in your new language.

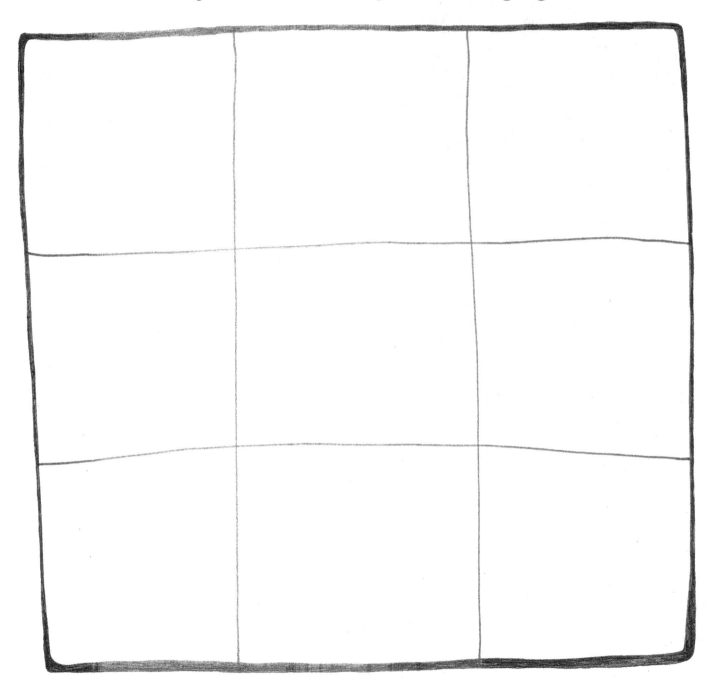

After you've finished, read your comic aloud seven times.

Make Your Own Texts

Using inspiration from the previous pages, make your own text conversation in your new language.

After you've finished, read your conversation aloud seven times.

MOVIE TIME!

Watch a film, documentary, or YouTube video in your new language

Title: ....
....
Producer: ....
....
Actors: ....
....
....

10 WORDS

Write down 10 words you hear while watching the film.

Foreign Language   **English**

1. _____   1. _____
2. _____   2. _____
3. _____   3. _____
4. _____   4. _____
5. _____   5. _____
6. _____   6. _____
7. _____   7. _____
8. _____   8. _____
9. _____   9. _____
10. _____   10. _____

RATING:

The Best

Amazing

Great

Good

Nice

Ok

Bad

Horrible

The Worst

EMERGENCIES
10 NEW WORDS!

Use a book, video, or Google Translate to find your ten words.

Foreign Language	English
_____	_____
_____	_____
_____	_____
_____	_____
_____	_____
_____	_____
_____	_____
_____	_____
_____	_____
_____	_____

Research ten words you might use in a conversation about emergencies.

After you've written your words, say them each seven times out loud, picturing them in your mind.

Research Time!

FIVE NEW PHRASES!

Research five phrases you might use in a conversation about emergencies.

1. __Foreign Language_____

   __English_____

   _____

2. _____

   _____

   _____

3. _____

   _____

   _____

4. _____

   _____

   _____

5. _____

   _____

After you've written your phrases, say them each seven times out loud, picturing them in your mind.

The Fun Page

EMOTIONAL TALK: Worry

Write down ten words that you might use when you're worried.

Foreign Language	English
1._____	1._____
2._____	2._____
3._____	3._____
4._____	4._____
5._____	5._____
6._____	6._____
7._____	7._____
8._____	8._____
9._____	9._____
10._____	10._____

After you've written your words, say them each seven times out loud, picturing them in your mind.

Illustrate what you've learned.

Make Your Own Comic

Using inspiration from the previous pages, make your own comic in _____ .

After you've finished, read your comic aloud seven times.

Make Your Own Texts

Using inspiration from the previous pages, make your own text conversation in _____ .

After you've finished, read your conversation aloud seven times.

MOVIE TIME!

Watch a film, documentary, or YouTube video in your new language

Title: ....
....
Producer: ....
....
Actors: ....
....
....

10 WORDS

Write down 10 words you hear while watching the film.

Foreign Language

1. _____
2. _____
3. _____
4. _____
5. _____
6. _____
7. _____
8. _____
9. _____
10. _____

English

1. _____
2. _____
3. _____
4. _____
5. _____
6. _____
7. _____
8. _____
9. _____
10. _____

RATING:

The Best

Amazing

Great

Good

Nice

Ok

Bad

Horrible

The Worst

PEOPLE
10 NEW WORDS!

Use a book, video, or Google Translate to find your ten words.

Foreign Language	English
_____	_____
_____	_____
_____	_____
_____	_____
_____	_____
_____	_____
_____	_____
_____	_____
_____	_____
_____	_____

Research ten words you might use in a conversation about people.

After you've written your words, say them each seven times out loud, picturing them in your mind.

Research Time!

FIVE NEW PHRASES!

Research five phrases you might use in a conversation about people.

1. **Foreign Language** _____

    English _____

2. _____

3. _____

4. _____

5. _____

After you've written your phrases, say them each seven times out loud, picturing them in your mind.

The Fun Page

EMOTIONAL TALK: Excitement

Write down five phrases you might use when you're excited.

1. Foreign Language _____
    English _____

2. _____
   _____

3. _____
   _____

4. _____
   _____

5. _____
   _____

After you've written these sentences, say them each seven times out loud, picturing them in your mind.

Illustrate what you've learned.

Make Your Own Comic

Using inspiration from the previous pages, make your own comic in your new language.

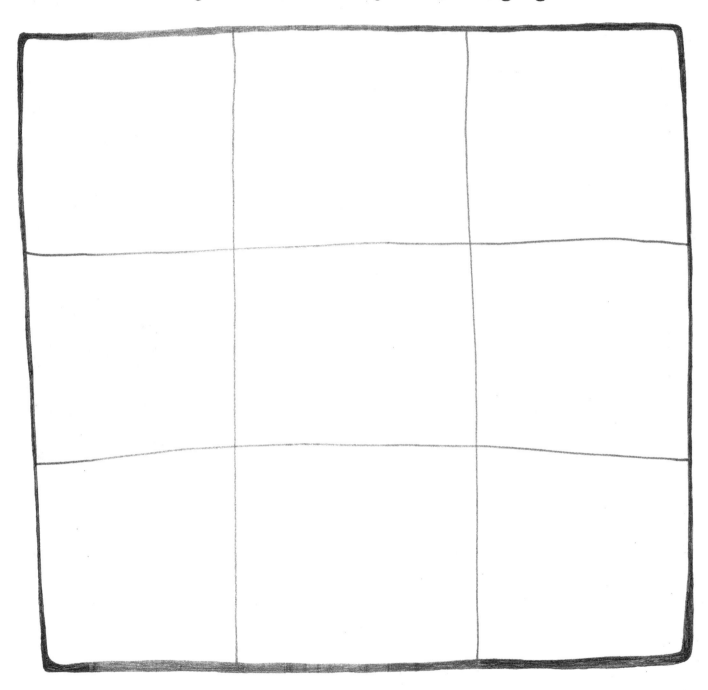

After you've finished, read your comic aloud seven times.

Add Words to the Doodle

**Find words to describe this picture.
Add your words to this page in a creative way.**

MOVIE TIME!

Watch a film, documentary, or YouTube video in your new language

Title: ....
....
Producer: ....
....
Actors: ....
....
....

10 WORDS

Write down 10 words you hear while watching the film.

Foreign Language

1. _____
2. _____
3. _____
4. _____
5. _____
6. _____
7. _____
8. _____
9. _____
10. _____

English

1. _____
2. _____
3. _____
4. _____
5. _____
6. _____
7. _____
8. _____
9. _____
10. _____

RATING:

The Best

Amazing

Great

Good

Nice

Ok

Bad

Horrible

The Worst

FITNESS
10 NEW WORDS!

> Use a book, video, or Google Translate to find your ten words.

Foreign Language	English
_____	_____
_____	_____
_____	_____
_____	_____
_____	_____
_____	_____
_____	_____
_____	_____
_____	_____
_____	_____

Research ten words you might use in a conversation about fitness.

> After you've written your words, say them each seven times out loud, picturing them in your mind.

Research Time!

FIVE NEW PHRASES!

Research five phrases you might use in a conversation about fitness.

1. Foreign Language _____
   English _____

2. _____
   _____

3. _____
   _____

4. _____
   _____

5. _____
   _____

After you've written your phrases, say them each seven times out loud, picturing them in your mind.

The Fun Page

What do you want to learn to say?

Write down five phrases that you'd like to learn.

1. _Foreign Language_____
   _English_____

2. _____
   _____

3. _____
   _____

4. _____
   _____

5. _____
   _____

After you've written these sentences, say them each seven times out loud, picturing them in your mind.

Illustrate what you've learned.

Make Your Own Comic

Using inspiration from the previous pages,
make your own comic in _____ .

After you've finished, read your comic aloud seven times.

Add Words to the Doodle

**Find words to describe this picture.
Add your words to this page in a creative way.**

The End!

Look though this book!

Find all your favorite words.

Doodle them here:

What is Fun-Schooling?

Fun-schooling is a one-of-a-kind way to learn. It is tapping into kids' interests while covering all the major subjects. Fun-schooling is for creative learners, students with learning disabilities, gifted students, and everyone in between. It's a way for students to learn without the stress, pressure, and boredom of other methods. We started out creating materials for our children. Then friends and family wanted to try it out. Before we knew it, Fun-schooling with Thinking Tree Books was born!

Fun-Schooling With Thinking Tree Books

Copyright Information:

Thinking Tree Fun-Schooling Books and electronic printable downloads are for home and family use only. You may make copies of these materials for only the children in your household.

All other uses of this material must be permitted in writing by The Thinking Tree LLC. It is a violation of copyright law to distribute the electronic files or make copies for your friends, associates, or students without our permission. For information on using these materials for businesses, co-ops, summer camps, day camps, daycares, afterschool programs, churches, or schools, please contact us for licensing.

Contact Us:

Thinking Tree LLC
+1 (USA)   317.622.8852

info@funschooling.com

Made in the USA
Middletown, DE
12 August 2024

58949190R10124